TEXTURES

A PHOTOGRAPHIC ALBUM
FOR ARTISTS AND DESIGNERS

Phil Brodatz

DOVER PUBLICATIONS, INC.
Mineola, New York

TO LILLIAN for her patience and understanding

Bibliographical Note

This Dover edition, first published in 1999, is an unabridged and unaltered republication of the work originally published by Dover Publications, Inc., New York, in 1966.
Photographic prints of any of the illustrations in this book may be purchased by writing to Judith Brodatz Wolfsohn, 9954 S.W. 82nd Street, Miami, Florida 33173.

DOVER *Pictorial Archive* SERIES

Library of Congress Cataloging-in-Publication Data

Brodatz, Phil.
    Textures : a photographic album for artists and designers / Phil Brodatz.
        p.   cm.
    Originally published: 1966.
    ISBN 0-486-40699-7 (pbk.)
    1. Photography, Artistic.   2. Texture (Art)   I. Title.
TR650.B69   1999
779—dc21
                                        99-28805
                                            CIP

Manufactured in the United States of America
Dover Publications, Inc., 31 East 2nd Street, Mineola, N.Y. 11501

LIST OF PLATES

TEXTURES

An age of photography is likely to be an age of texture. With photographic skills and processes currently reaching an excellence little dreamed of fifty years ago, it is hardly surprising that our generation has taken a simultaneous interest in the look, touch, and feel of the world about us—an interest reflected in our clothing, our house furnishings, the very textures of our walls and the paintings we hang there.

The origins of what I have come to call Texturama came about, however, not through aesthetic speculation but through the difficulties of a photographic assignment. As a professional photographer whose work is often carried out according to the specifications of art directors and designers, I have frequently been asked to supply photographic backgrounds of different kinds—told to photograph water, clouds, or flowers, for example, against whose features could then be projected a sponsor's name or product.

Water, clouds, and flowers, however, are subjects that do not easily sit for their portraits. In contrast to the still-lifes I had been used to photographing, in which each aspect of lighting, background, and subject had been carefully arranged for maximum simplicity and effect, these were subjects that were in a constant state of motion and Heraclitean flux. Photograph them at morning and they would be completely different from the same objects viewed at noon.

Even an object in itself stationary—a chunk of granite, say, on a fence post on a sunny afternoon—would vary according to how and when it had been seen. Walk around the chunk of granite studying each of its sides and it would present a dozen different faces, as the angle, direction and intensity of the light varied. The same simple piece of stone would exhibit a myriad of different shades of gray, depending upon the nature and intensity of the light source.

It occurred to me that, for certain objects, rather than taking a shot or two and hoping for one that might be "best," it might be better to photograph them over a long period of time, perhaps at different seasons of the year or under quite different lighting conditions. The various shots could then be com-

VII

pared and the most useful selected for whatever project was at hand. When enough prints had been accumulated, there would be a reasonable basis for examination and comparison and decisions concerning future work.

My reasoning, after all, was nothing but taking account of one of our natural laws of light: that which hypothesizes that the color and tonal value of any substance are determined by the reflection of the light source. Accordingly I took the first of what I would later call Texturama shots, hoping to obtain more than simply a photograph. What I dared hope for were photographs with depth, with highlights and shadows that would give a deep-textured effect which, if successful, would make one want to reach out and touch the print.

The first results were well received. Art directors and designers, seeing them, were delighted with the patterns revealed; often they were surprised when told what the subject was. "Try water," I was told. "Try sand." "How would brick look?" "Try wood grains." I set out, hopefully, to do so, hardly knowing that my life had just taken a very decisive turn—that from one subject I would be led to another and another until finally I would have hundreds of three-dimensional prints on file and be on the lookout for texture in everything. As a result, two other things happened: I became much more aware of design in nature and, perhaps most important, became more alive to the possibilities of photography itself.

The professional photographer, after all, works usually within certain definite restrictions. There is the awareness he must have of the processes of graphic reproduction: he is forever at the mercy of the uncompromising dictates of reproducibility. He is, furthermore, always carrying out someone else's wishes, translating an art director's ideas into dramatic photographic illustrations. Assign him a proportion of 8½ by 11 and tell him the illustration must extend to the edge of the page, or bleed, and he will compose his work accordingly; tell him there will be a dropout or surprint, and further adjustments will be made.

There is nothing wrong with such restrictions; often they make the work more challenging, forcing the photographer to be creative within the limits allowed. But there are times one simply wishes to explore for the sake of exploring. Like the scientist, whose curiosity is held captive by the smallest dripping faucet or dried leaf till he has understood it, the photographer with today's outstanding tools at his command stands looking about him wondering "How would this photograph, or that? What would a window screen look like, properly lighted and magnified? How would burlap look, or cork, or a smooth grass lawn?" Out of such seemingly useless speculations have grown many useful things, including most of the photographs in this book. Among the further subjects that suggested themselves were woolen cloth, raffia weave, canvas, rice paper, netting, lace, brass mesh, marble, ceiling tile, reptile skin, pigskin, calfskin, calf leather, beach sand, straw, pebbles, soap bubbles, crushed rose quartz, and ice crystals. The results of many of these attempts may be seen on the following pages.

When enough Texturama prints had been made and the results could be compared, the second discovery asserted itself: that of design in nature. The subject is one that has intrigued minds as different as those of Aristotle, Roger Bacon, Leonardo, and Emerson. From Holmes' "chambered nautilus" to Hopkins' "dappled things," poets have been struck by the similarities of natural objects, as have painters from Brueghel to Monet. To attempt to say anything new on the matter would be foolish, but one is struck, in print after print, with patterns revealed by the very impersonality of photography. Thus one sees the nearly perfect little wirelike mesh on the snake's back, or the perfect, regular ovals of both sand dunes and rings on a tree.

It is hardly surprising if the patterns, once revealed, begin to suggest others. Thus a photograph of a simple Westchester County fieldstone may, upon scrutiny, suggest a painting of a choppy sea. Bubbles may seem to be marble. Calfskin appears to be papier-mâché, or the patterns of a swinging light bulb the delicate filaments of dandelion seed. Why these patterns are revealed by photography more than to the naked eye has yet to be explained, but there is no doubt that many persons, seeing the Texturama prints, feel that they have seen the subject more truly, seen its form, how it is made. And that, at least, is part of what Texturama is all about.

2

A variety of methods was used to obtain the texture photographs shown in this volume. Most important, of course, was the distinction between outdoor and indoor shots.

For outdoor shots, two basic procedures were followed. There is the simple shot of clouds and water, which requires no preparation. One merely sees an interesting viewpoint, presenting a maximum of dramatic illustration, varies his film and filter, and takes the photograph.

Slightly more preparation is involved in the outdoor shot in which static materials are being used: straw on the beach, or sand or pebbles. These I photograph on location, using a six-foot ladder for overhead views and convenience stands for holding the materials motionless. One must be prepared to feel slightly foolish mounting a six-foot ladder with a 4 x 5 Speed Graphic or 5 x 7 View Camera on a huge wooden tripod appearing to be photographing nothing at all, but the results are worth any difficulties entailed. I find sunlight particularly interesting for many opaque materials, and for obvious reasons take most outdoor shots in spring and summer.

In the studio, one's approach can be quite different, for here one has many more conveniences to work with (see Figure 1 for studio setup). For those substances such as pellets, stones, and quartz which are best photographed from directly overhead, I use an 8 x 10 View Camera attached to a new floor-model drill stand. The camera is counterbalanced with weights to permit it to ride up and down easily.

I take many more shots than are necessary, in order to see the subtle differences that reveal themselves in the prints. Magnification can vary considerably; that for the prints in this volume varies from a magnification of four times actual size to a reduction of one-twelfth actual size.

Of primary importance, of course, is the question of lighting. For back lighting, I use a special twenty-four-inch square neon grid with a high-voltage transformer for power. This provides a flat even white ground, and is most effective for silhouetting a substance. A small distance above the grid is a white lucite panel to diffuse the grid light, and then a sheet of plate glass.

For front lighting I use one of the following: a 750-watt spotlight, a 1000-watt incandescent floodlight in a studio modeling reflector, a Sylvania Professional Sun Gun, or diffused daylight through the skylight.

Each of these light sources has a different quality. The incandescent flood, for example, has a soft diffused quality, so that the surface area is clearly seen, and its roundness shades gently with an open shadow. When the spotlight is used, on the other hand, the highlight is lighter and the roundness is sharply delineated with a deeper, darker shadow. To dramatize the form of the subject, however, I prefer the straight, brilliant rays of the Sun Gun. When this

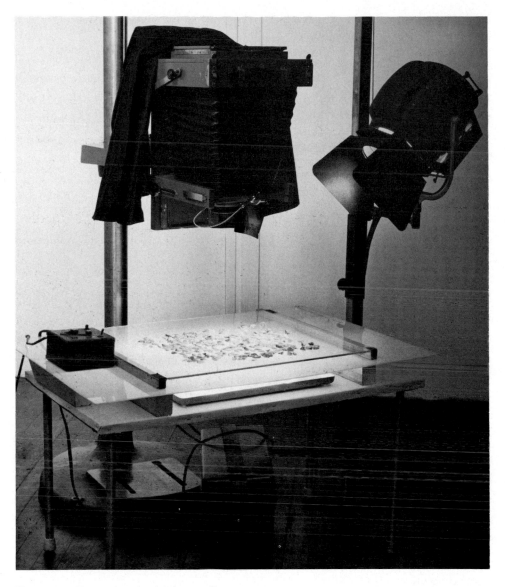

Figure 1   Camera setup in the studio.

is used, one has a bright, hard shape to the highlight area, and a sharp black shadow, with virtually no tone or detail in the highlight area or in the shadow area (see Plates D74 and D75, for the lighting of coffee beans).

For any one photograph, of course, considerable variation is possible, as can be seen from the captions in this volume, which range from bright crosslighting to balanced fluorescent light, illuminated background, shadowgraph, electronic flash, bright or diffused sunlight, and many others.

The principal source of this variation is, of course, the balance achieved between front light and back light. Here small changes will sometimes result in marked differences in the prints. In some, the most interesting shapes will reveal themselves in the highlight area; in others, the interest will reside in the shape of the shadow.

For those who find such terms as "highlight" and "shadow" confusing, consider the following: Think of everything in terms of white, black, and grays in between. If you were to represent such an arrangement on a light chart, white would be at the top as the lightest and brightest, and black at the bottom as the darkest. With only these two represented, one would have maximum separation or greatest contrast.

Most of the time, however, one has to deal with many tones of gray, in between the extremes of black and white; and to understand these it may help to carry out the following demonstration. Place, say, an elementary form on a table—a ball, cylinder, or cube. Light it with a single light source and look at it with one eye. You would then be looking at its forward side, and have somewhat the same relationship to it as that which exists between the film and the object being photographed.

Now "see" the shape of the form as white, and see it outlined in black. If the shape is only white and it is outlined in white, it has minimum contrast and one can hardly find the shape; in photography this is referred to as "high-key," as opposed to the maximum contrast mentioned above.

If now we look at the cylinder (using always only one eye), we will see the whitest light, or highlight. This is the point closest to the light source, and shadings will be gray as we descend to the outside of the object. It is this gradation of grays which gives a sense of curvature or roundness to the cylinder or ball.

The shape of the highlight further identifies the material from which the object is made. Wood, clay, and the like, have a soft diffused highlight. Glass, steel, and chrome have a hard sharp highlight.

Finally, look at the black area, or shadow (again using only one eye). It is this which outlines the shape of the object. In the case of the three-dimensional object mentioned above—the ball, cylinder, or cube—the shadow would also give us a clue to its depth. If we had used two eyes to look at the object, we would have had the additional sense of depth resulting from stereo-scopic vision.

In looking at any object, therefore, we have these factors: a white (high-light), a sense of shape in the grays, which in turn descend to a black (shadow). When there is detail visible in the shadow, we refer to it as an open shadow (in contrast to the closed, or completely dark, shadow).

These basic principles of lighting apply to everything you will ever look at or photograph, and can be seen at work in the photographs in this book.

3

What are the uses of Texturama, and what potentialities for development does it have? Since the process grew initially out of a photographic assignment, it is not surprising that it suggests many commercial uses. The prints can be used as backgrounds for printed art, or to cover broad areas of printed sheets with an interesting effect. They can provide bleed borders for full-page advertise-ments. Texturama prints have been successfully adapted to lettering, or to spe-cialized laboratory processes. Small objects—whether a sponsor's product or trade name or some other device—can be placed on them and then photo-graphed.

The art director or designer, furthermore, may use such a collection as a reference—looking through the pages, examining photographs for pattern and tone, to find exactly the right effect, contrast, or value for the particular re-quirements of the job at hand. Photographers may find the prints will suggest new areas in their work, as will perhaps painters, designers, and decorators.

The uses by the general reader will be less commercial but, it is hoped, no less real. For he may simply browse, enjoying the prints for what they are, searching for patterns that somehow elude the untrained eye until they are brought to a still point and photographed.

To see the world in a grain of sand has been man's hope long before Blake put it into words. It is possible to do so, but it requires assistance. The scien-tist must instruct us in the laws governing sand; the philosopher must relate these to the universe at large. In this process of seeing or understanding, the photographer, though he little dreams of it, has a role to play. He can show us the sand so that we see a world there.

Our generation has been lucky in this. Thanks to black-and-white and color photography and motion pictures, we have probably seen the world more closely than the people of any earlier period. But the world we have seen has not been the romantic landscape of the nineteenth century; it has been the world seen close, in detail, the structure of things as they are.

All of this suggests one of the two possible developments of texture photography: its relationship with scientific photography and photomicrography. These fields, which have expanded immensely in our time, will undoubtedly benefit from developments in any other area of photography itself.

Whether, as has been generously suggested, texture photography can proceed in the other direction—that of art—and develop as the basis of an art form, cannot easily be said. It is too soon to know, but any development in that direction would surely not be amiss.

Such photography would, at any rate, offer two advantages to the photographer who undertakes it. It requires, first, no special subject matter or travel on the part of the photographer. He can do as well photographing the familiar stones of his back yard as he can the steps of the pyramids. And one further advantage: I see no immediate possibility of the exhaustion of subject matter. One can go on forever photographing clouds, trees, bricks, hillsides, beaches, pebbles, walls, wood, cement—whatever is at hand—and always with fresh results. Even what has been photographed many times before can be shot again—from a new angle and with new lighting. There is no end to it; rather, it is the other way around: the more we become aware of textures, the more we see. What had seemed an uninteresting, flat concrete wall suddenly becomes something quite different because of a trick in the lighting, a small ripple in the surface perhaps, something we see because of its relation to our past work. One small defect may give it a new face. And come back in an hour and it will have another.

If the texture photographs in this book actually have this effect—of making any part of the world seem new—that is satisfaction enough. They show us only what is all around us, if we will only look and see.

D1   Woven aluminum wire.
Classical lighting; spotlight from upper left. Magnification 8 x.

D2   Fieldstone (Westchester County).
Photographed in bright sunlight. Actual size.

D3   Reptile skin.
Spotlight. Magnification 2 x.

D4 Pressed cork.
Crosslighting in sunlight. Slightly enlarged.

D5   Expanded mica.
Photographed in daylight. Magnification 3 x.

D6   Woven aluminum wire.
Light paper background; photographed in sunlight.
Magnification 2 x.

D7   Fieldstone (Westchester County).
Photographed in bright sunlight. Actual size.

D8   Abstract illusion of woven wire.
Magnification 8 x.

D9   Grass lawn.
Photographed in sunlight.

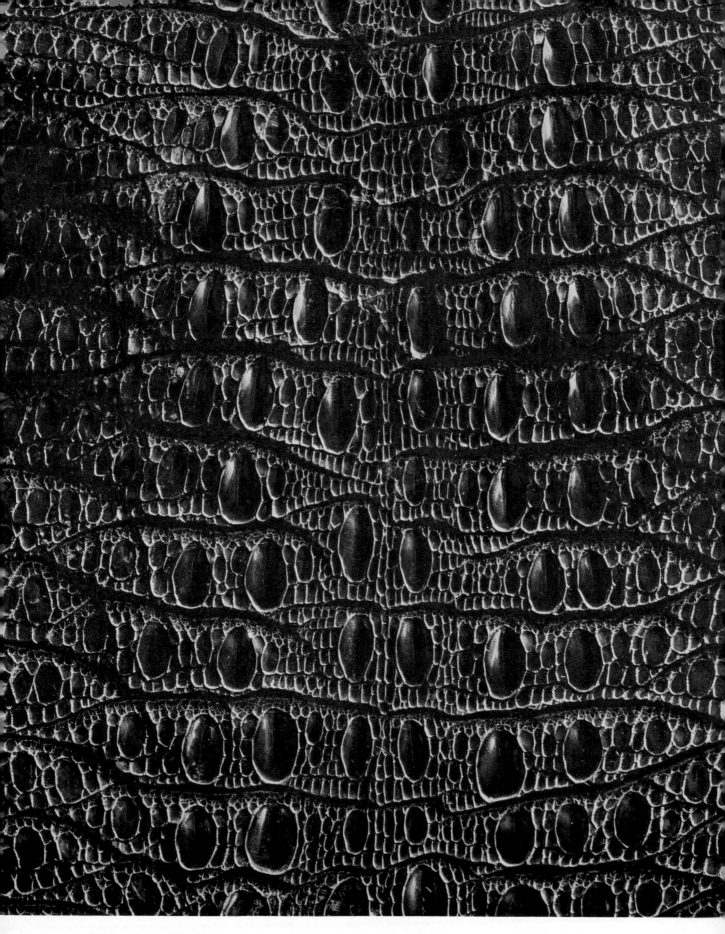

D10   Crocodile skin.
Spotlight. Magnification 2 x.

D11   Homespun woolen cloth.
Flat studio lighting; balanced on both sides. Actual size.

D12   Bark of tree.
Photographed in morning sunlight. Reduced to ½ actual size.

D13   Bark of tree.
Photographed in sunlight. Magnification 2 x.

D14　Woven aluminum wire.
Dark paper background; crosslighting. Magnification 4 x.

D15   Straw (North Shore beach, Long Island).
Overhead view; photographed in sunlight.

D16   Herringbone weave.
Balanced studio lighting. Actual size.

D17   Herringbone weave.
Balanced studio lighting. Magnification 4 x.

D18   Raffia weave.
Balanced studio lighting. Magnification 1½ x.

D19   Woolen cloth, loosely woven with soft tufts.
Flat lighting. Magnification 1½ x.

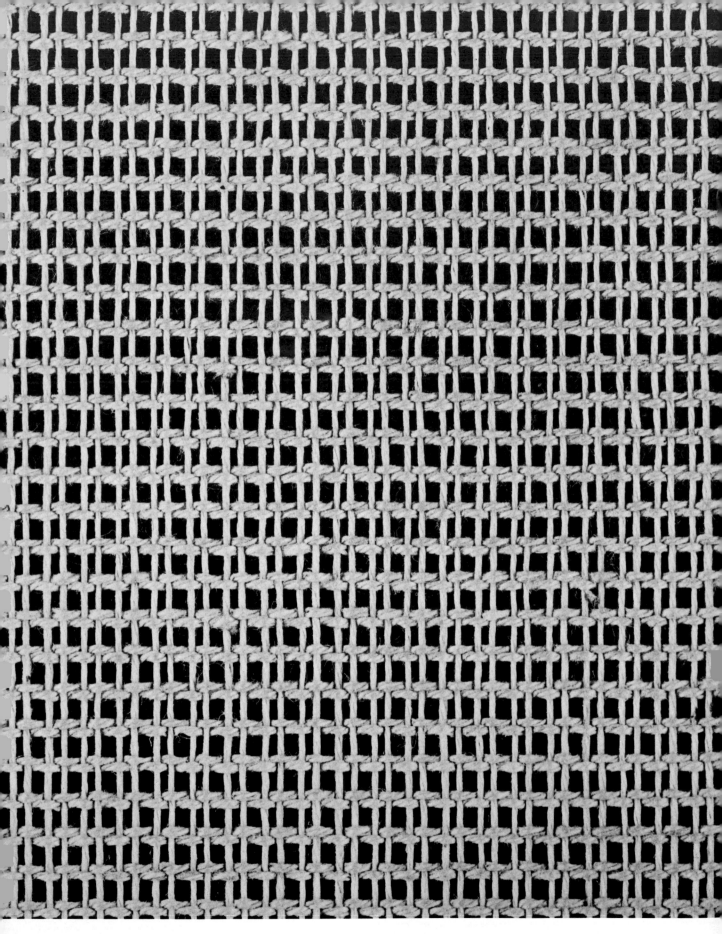

D20   French canvas.
Balanced fluorescent lighting. Magnification 4 x.

D21 French canvas.
Balanced front lighting on black background.
Reduced to ½ actual size.

D22   Reptile skin.
Photographed in sunlight. Magnification 2 x.

D23   Beach pebbles.
Photographed in diffused sunlight. Slightly reduced.

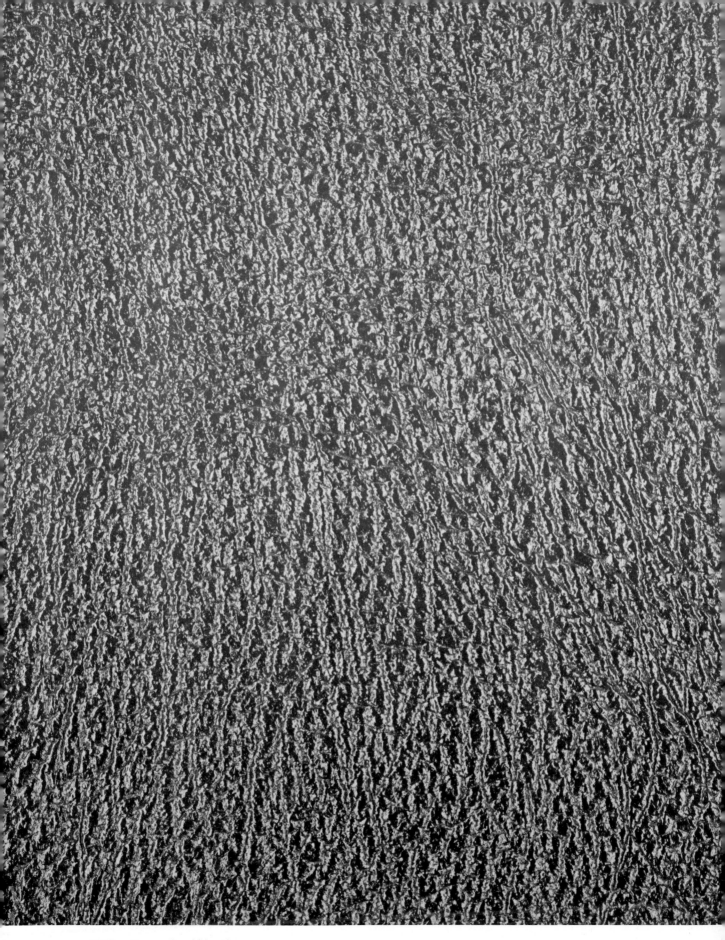

D24   Pressed calf leather.
Bright crosslighting. Magnification 2 x.

D25   Ceramic-coated brick wall.
Photographed in soft sunlight. Reduced to ½ actual size.

D26   Ceramic-coated brick wall.
Photographed in daylight. Reduced to ¼ actual size.

D27   Beach sand and pebbles—translucent effect.
Photographed in diffused sunlight. Slightly reduced.

D28 Beach sand.
Photographed in sunlight. Magnification 4 x.

D29 Beach sand.
Photographed in sunlight. Slightly enlarged.

D30   Beach pebbles—translucent effect.
Photographed in sunlight. Magnification 2 x.

D31 Beach pebbles with hard, dry appearance.
Photographed in bright sunlight. Magnification 2 x.

D32   Pressed cork.
Balanced studio lighting. Reduced to ½ actual size.

D33   Pressed cork.
Balanced studio lighting. Magnification 1½ x.

D34   Netting.
Photographed on rear illuminated unit. Magnification 4 x.

D35   Lizard skin.
Balanced studio lighting. Magnification 2 x.

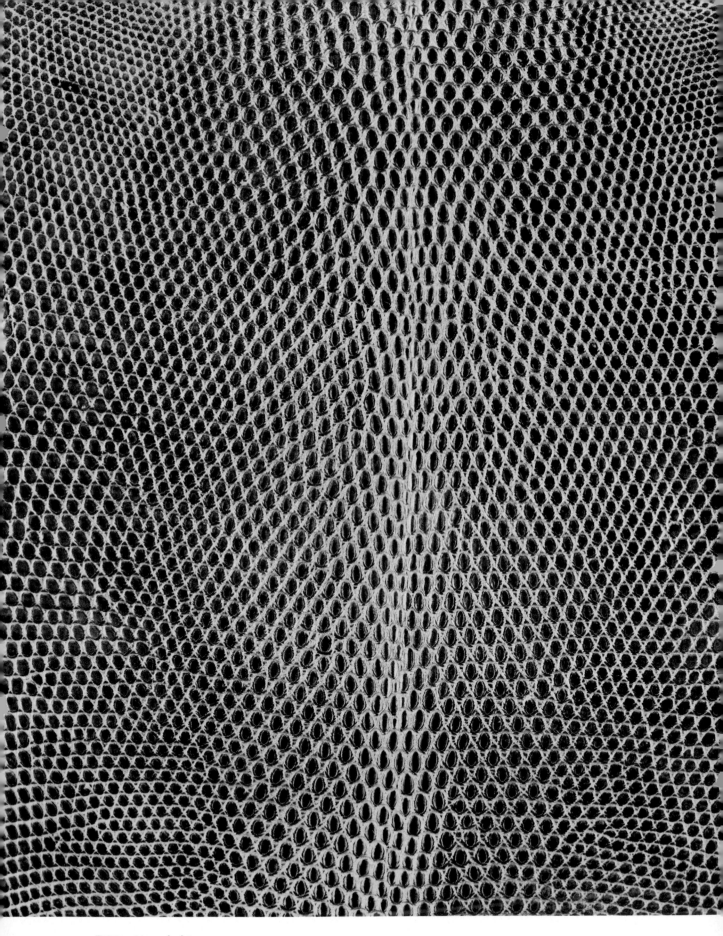

D36   Lizard skin.
Balanced studio lighting. Slightly enlarged.

D37   Water.
Wave pattern detail; photographed in sunlight.
Reduced to ⅓ actual size.

D38 Water.
View of wind and wave patterns.

D39   Lace.
Crosslighting for relief effect. Actual size.

D40 Lace.
Stitch detail in flower pattern. Balanced studio lighting and
rear illumination. Actual size.

D41   Lace.
Fine stitch detail. Photographed against illuminated background.
Magnification 1½ x.

D42 Lace.
Fine separation of weave from background. Balanced studio
lighting. Magnification 1½ x.

D43   Varied swinging of light bulb on a length of wire
in a darkened room.

D44   Swinging lights in a darkened room. Arc about eight feet.

D45   Abstract effect of swinging light, with only one side of
bulb exposed. Reverse side seems to disappear.

D46   Woven brass mesh.
Focus is on shadow cast in background. Floodlight.
Magnification 2 x.

D47 Woven brass mesh.
Photographed in sunlight. Magnification 2 x.

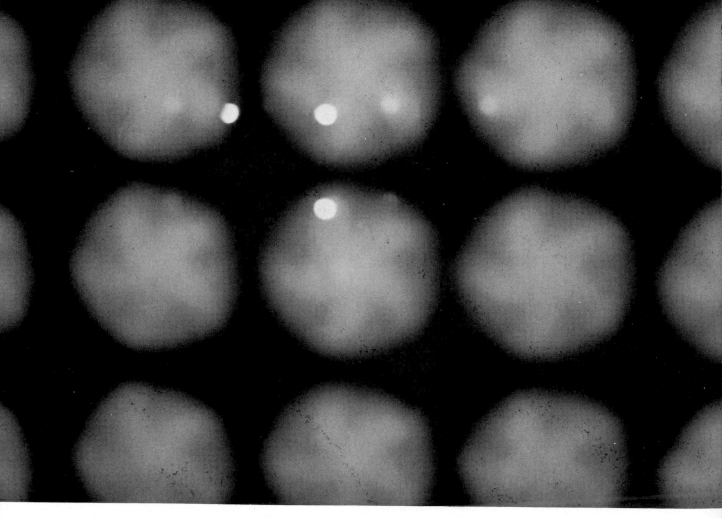

D48   Perforated masonite panel.
Back lighting with rays penetrating the openings.
Magnification 2 x.

D49   Straw screening.
Top lighting for high contrast silhouette effect. Actual size.

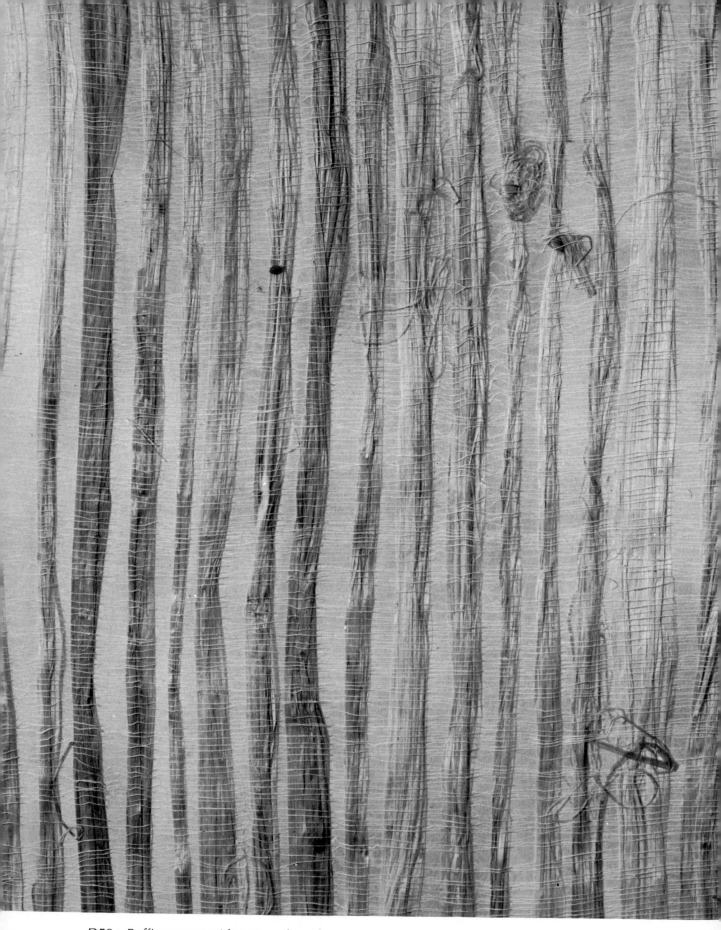

D50　Raffia woven with cotton threads.
Front lighting. Actual size.

D51   Raffia woven with cotton threads.
Back lighting. Magnification 1½ x.

D52 Oriental straw cloth.
Back and front lighting. Magnification 2 x.

D53 Oriental straw cloth.
Back and front lighting. Magnification 2 x.

D54   Beach pebbles.
High overhead view; photographed in evening sunlight.
Magnification ¼ x.

D55 Straw matting.
Flat lighting. Actual size.

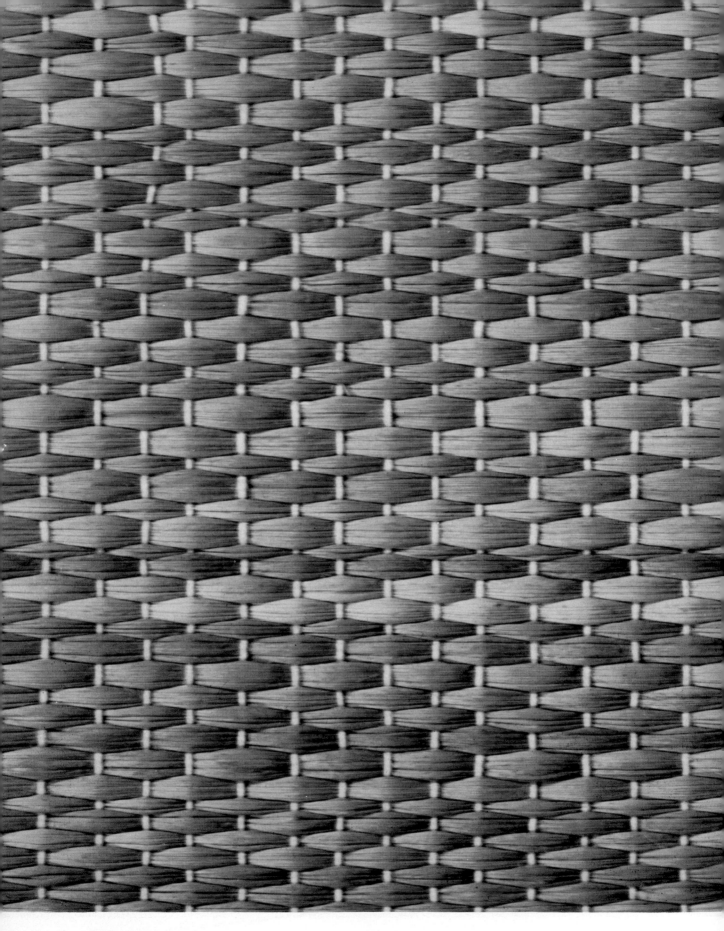

D56   Straw matting.
Balanced fluorescent lighting. Magnification 4 x.

D57 Handmade paper.
Hard crosslighting. Magnification 2 x.

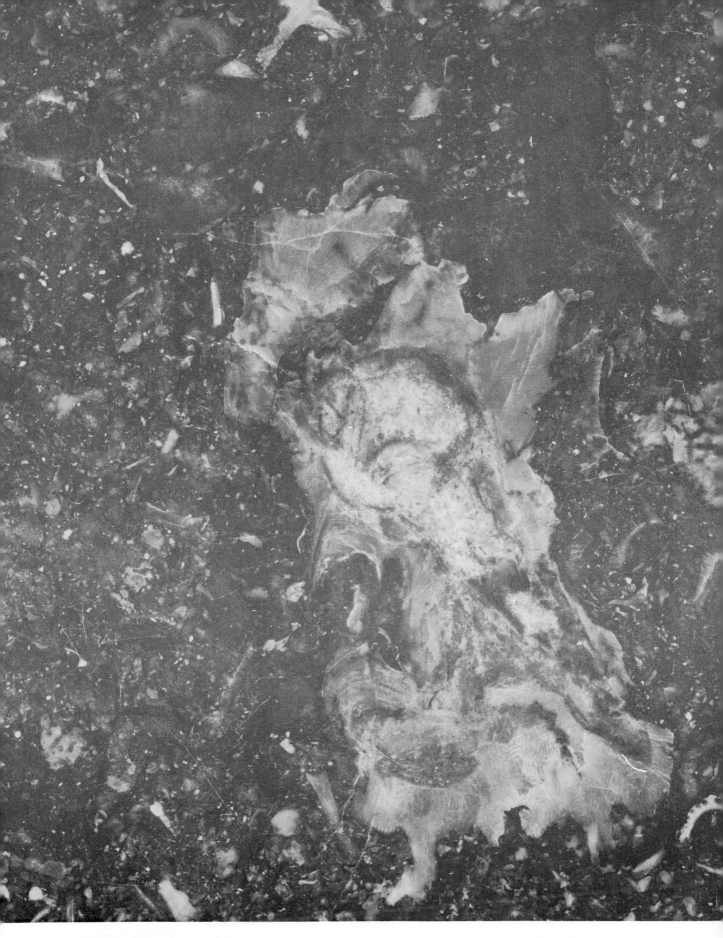

D58   European marble.
Balanced floodlighting. Actual size.

D59   European marble.
Balanced floodlighting. Magnification 2 x.

D60   European marble.
Balanced floodlighting. Actual size.

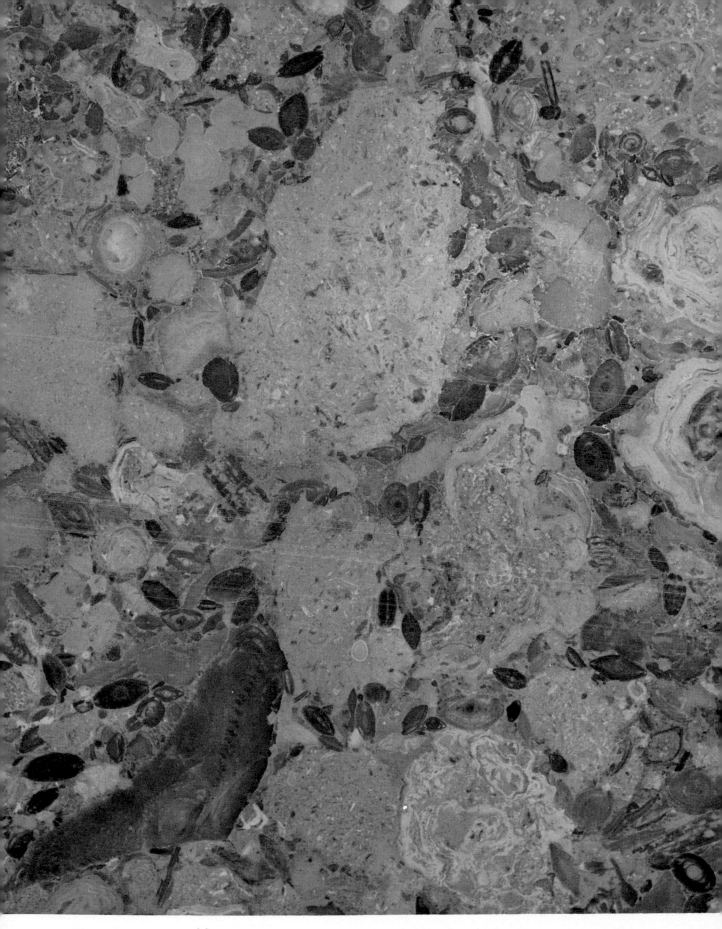

D61   European marble.
Balanced floodlighting. Actual size.

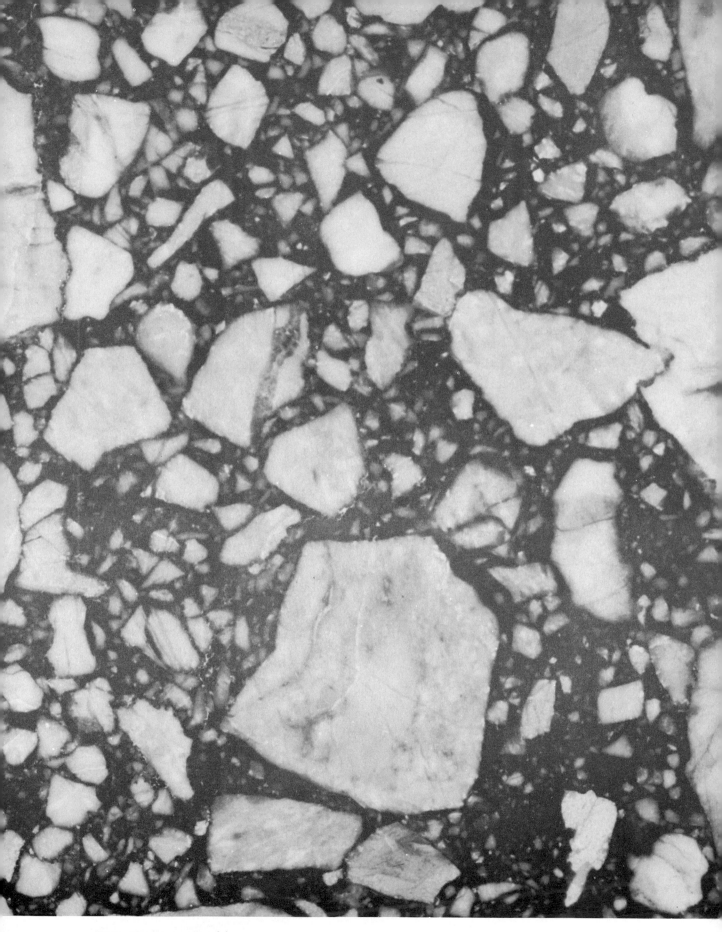

D62   European marble.
Balanced floodlighting. Magnification 3 x.

D63   European marble.
Balanced floodlighting. Actual size.

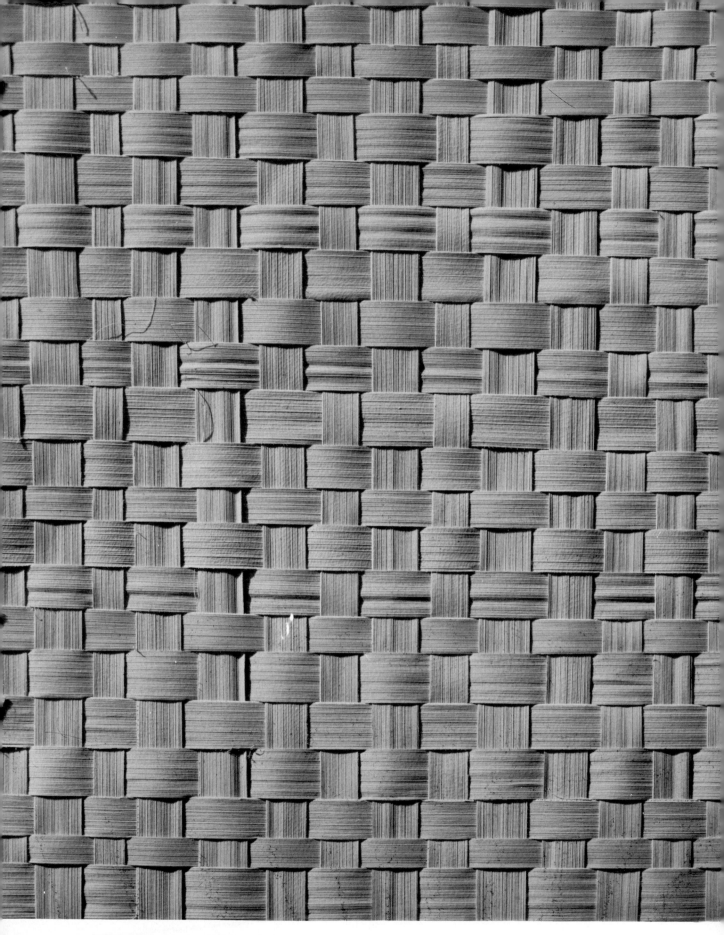

D64 Handwoven Oriental rattan.
Crosslighting in sunlight. Actual size.

D65   Handwoven Oriental rattan.
Photographed in sunlight. Actual size.

D66   Plastic pellets.
Soft incandescent lighting. Slightly enlarged.

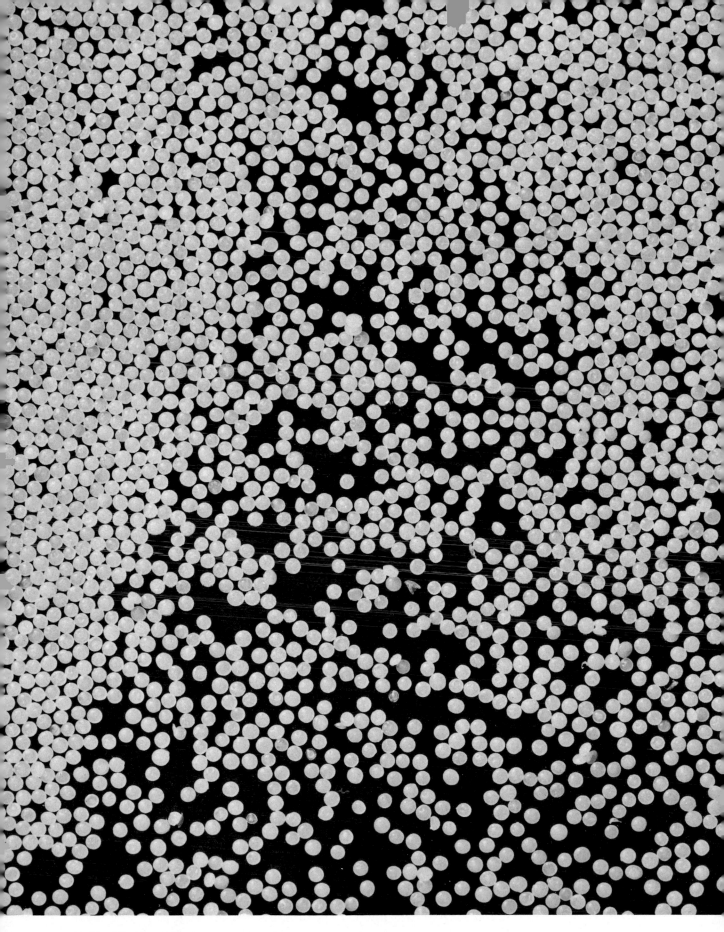

D67   Plastic pellets.
Single-source floodlight. Reduced to ⅓ actual size.

D68 Wood grain.
Balanced fluorescent lighting. Magnification 2 x.

D69　Wood grain.
Balanced fluorescent lighting. Magnification 2 x.

D70   Wood grain.
Balanced fluorescent lighting. Magnification 2 x.

D71   Wood grain.
Balanced fluorescent lighting. Magnification 2 x.

D72   Tree stump, used as a chopping block.
Professional Sun Gun providing single light source in studio.
Actual size.

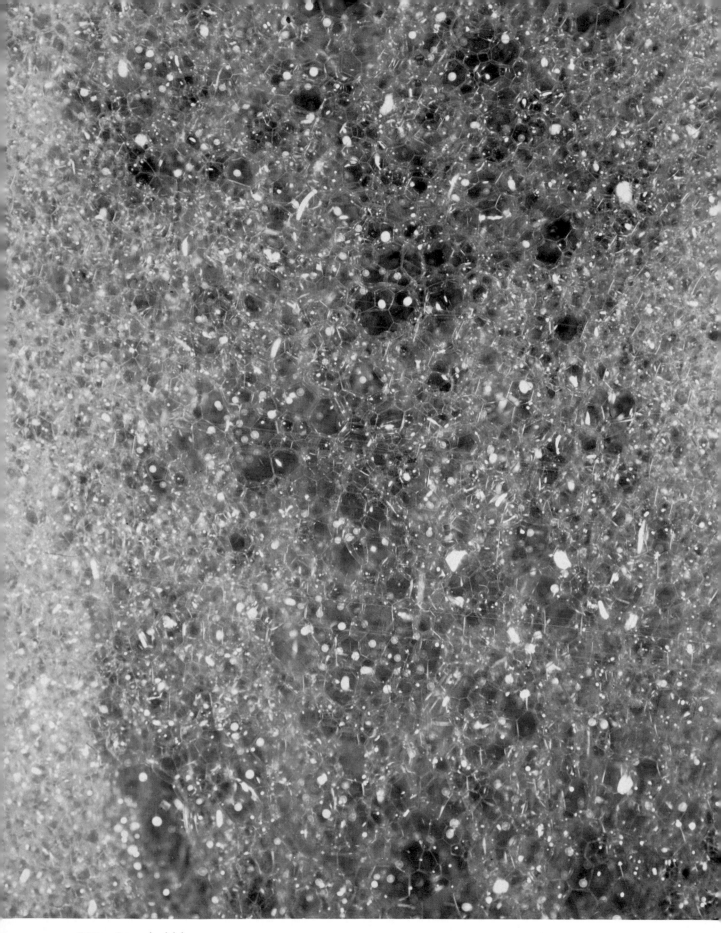

D73   Soap bubbles.
Stop motion with electronic flash. Actual size.

D74   Coffee beans.
Back and side lighting. Magnification 1¼ x.

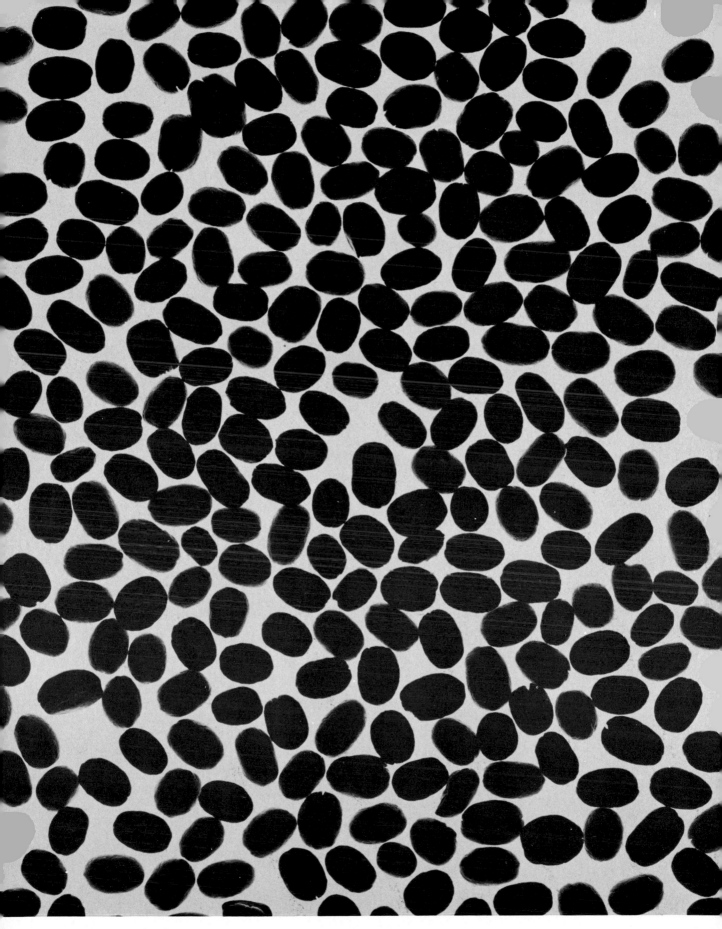

D75   Coffee beans.
Back lighting; medium speed Pan film. Slightly enlarged.

D76   Oriental grass fiber cloth.
Photographed in sunlight. Reduced to ½ actual size.

D77 Cotton canvas.
Photographed in sunlight. Magnification 1½ x.

D78 Oriental straw cloth.
Sunlight only as front lighting.

D79   Oriental grass fiber cloth.
Photographed in sunlight. Actual size.

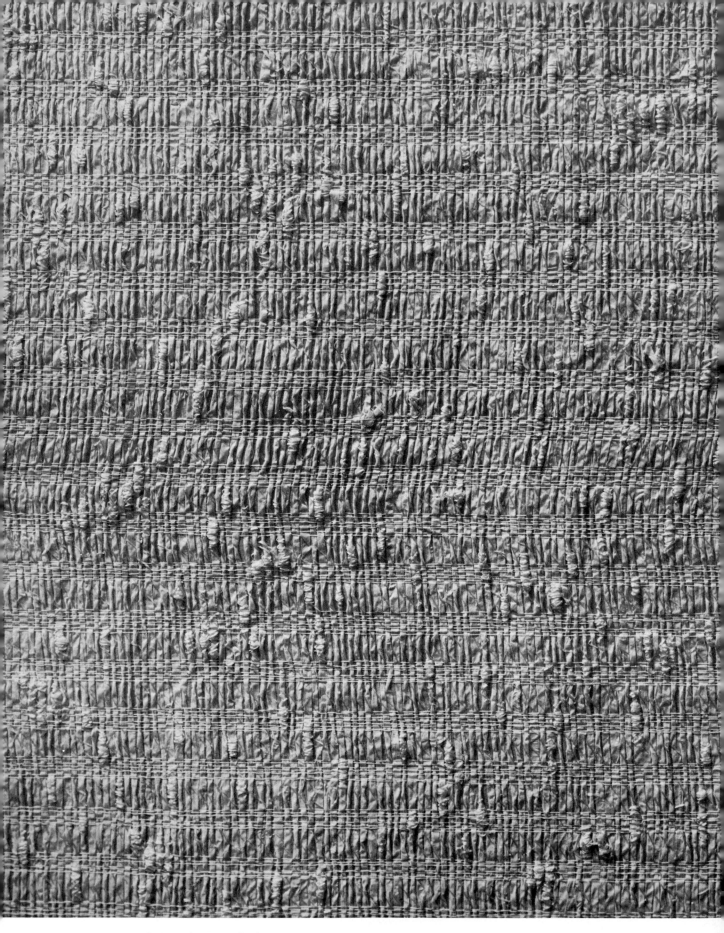

D80   Oriental straw cloth.
Sunlight only as front lighting.

D81   Oriental straw cloth.
Back lighting and strong crosslighting. Actual size.

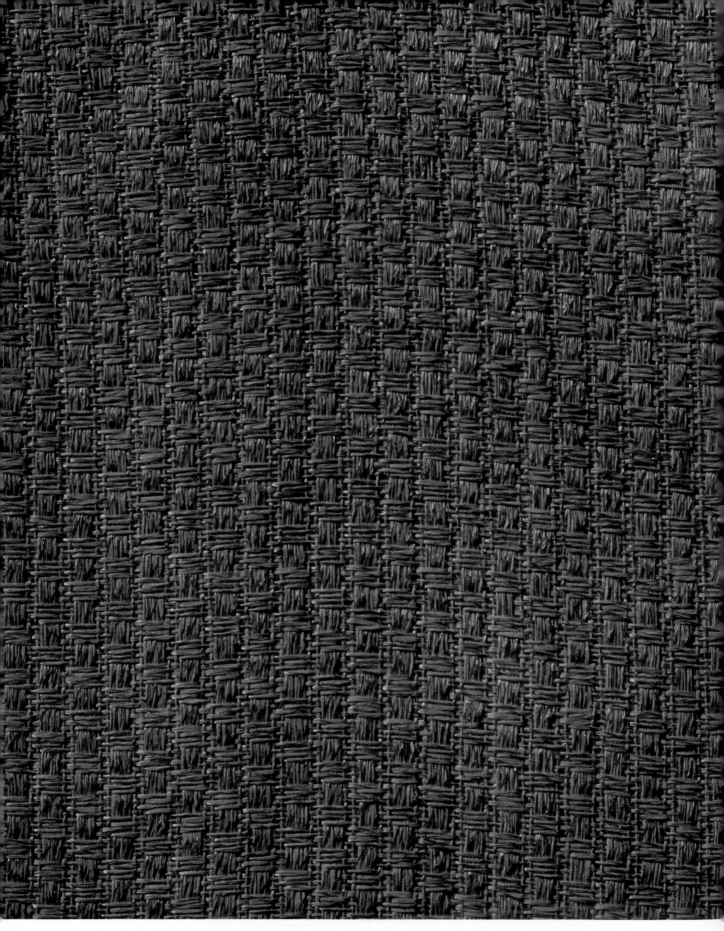

D82   Oriental straw cloth.
Photographed in sunlight. Actual size.

D83   Woven matting.
Photographed in sunlight. Actual size.

D84   Raffia looped to a high pile.
Photographed in sunlight. Actual size.

D85   Straw matting with bamboo effect.
Photographed in sunlight. Actual size.

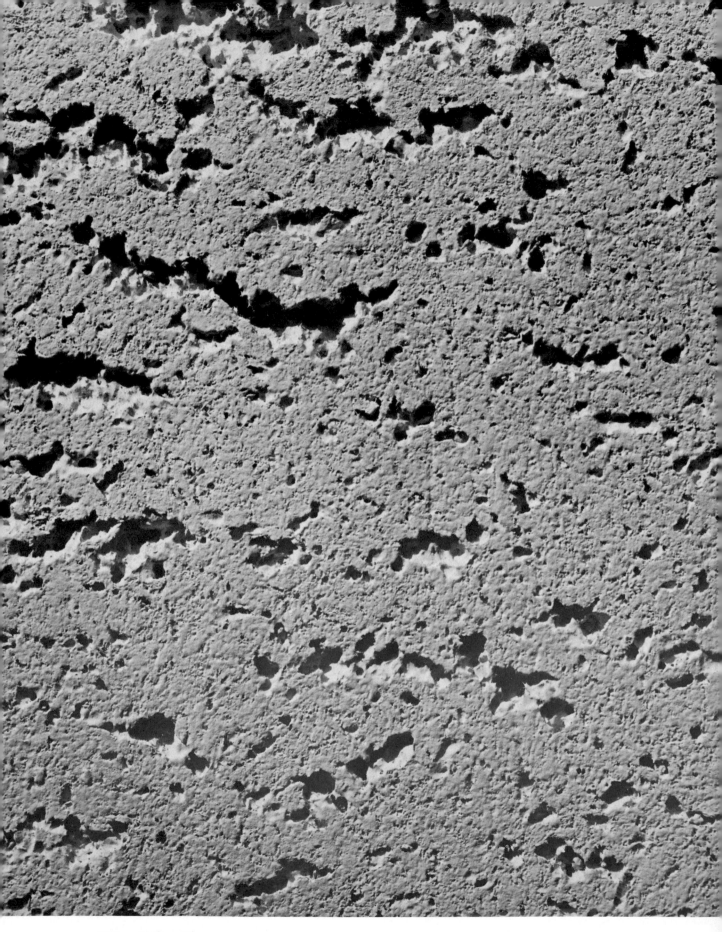

D86   Ceiling tile.
Photographed in bright sunlight. Magnification 2 x.

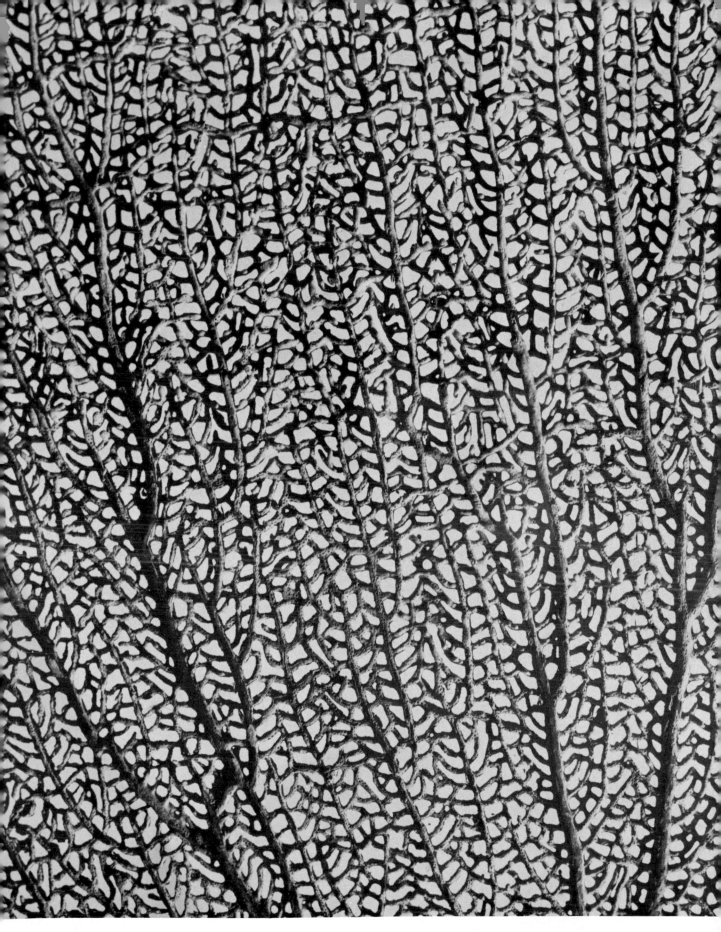

D87　Sea fan, fossilized with a coral covering.
Photographed in sunlight against a white card background.
Actual size.

D88   Dried hop flowers.
Back lighting with neon grid. Magnification 1½ x.

D89   Dried hop flowers.
Studio crosslighting with incandescent spot.
Magnification 1½ x.

D90　Clouds.
Medium yellow (G) filter on medium speed Pan film.

D91   Clouds.
Infra-red film with #29 filter.

D92 Pigskin.
Balanced studio lighting. Magnification 2 x.

D93   Fur. Hide of unborn calf.
Balanced studio lighting. Magnification 2 x.

D94   Brick wall.
Photographed in sunlight. Reduced to 1/6 actual size.

D95   Brick wall.
Photographed in sunlight. Reduced to 1/12 actual size.

D96   Brick wall.
Photographed in sunlight. Reduced to ¼ actual size.

D97   Cross section of a weathered tree stump.
Studio lighting with one Professional Sun Gun. Slightly enlarged.

D98   Crushed rose quartz.
Front lighting. Actual size.

D99   Crushed rose quartz.
Back lighting. Magnification 2 x.

D100   Ice crystals on an automobile.
Flashbulb used as a sidelight. Magnification 2 x.

D101   Cane.
Shadowgraph. Actual size.

D102   Cane.
Shadowgraph. Actual size.

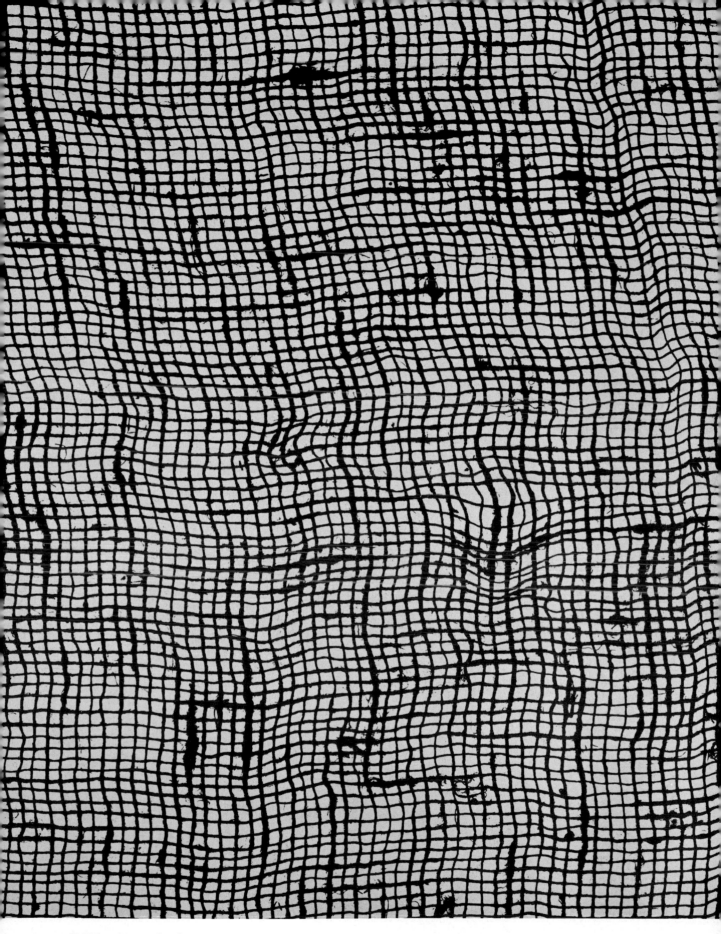

D103   Loose burlap.
Shadowgraph. Actual size.

D104   Loose burlap.
Shadowgraph. Actual size.

D105   Cheesecloth.
Shadowgraph. Actual size.

D106 Cheesecloth.
Shadowgraph. Actual size.

D107   Japanese rice paper.
Shadowgraph. Actual size.

D108   Japanese rice paper.
Shadowgraph. Actual size.

D109   Handmade paper, grassy fiber.
Shadowgraph. Actual size.

D110 · Handmade paper, grassy fiber.
Shadowgraph. Actual size.

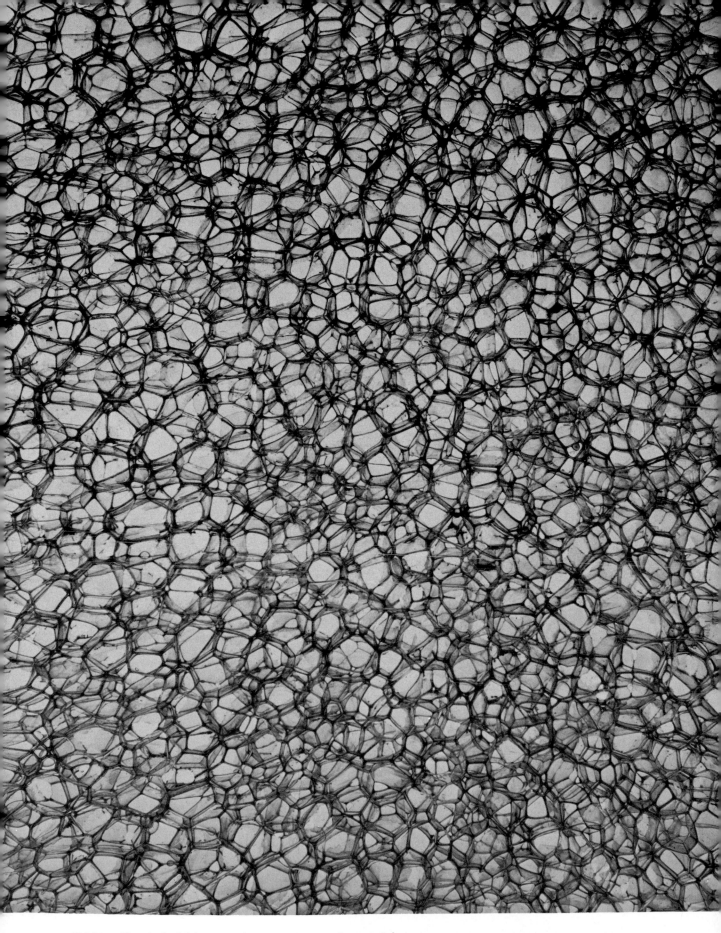

D111   Plastic bubbles, used as experimental material.
Back lighting. Reduced to ½ actual size.

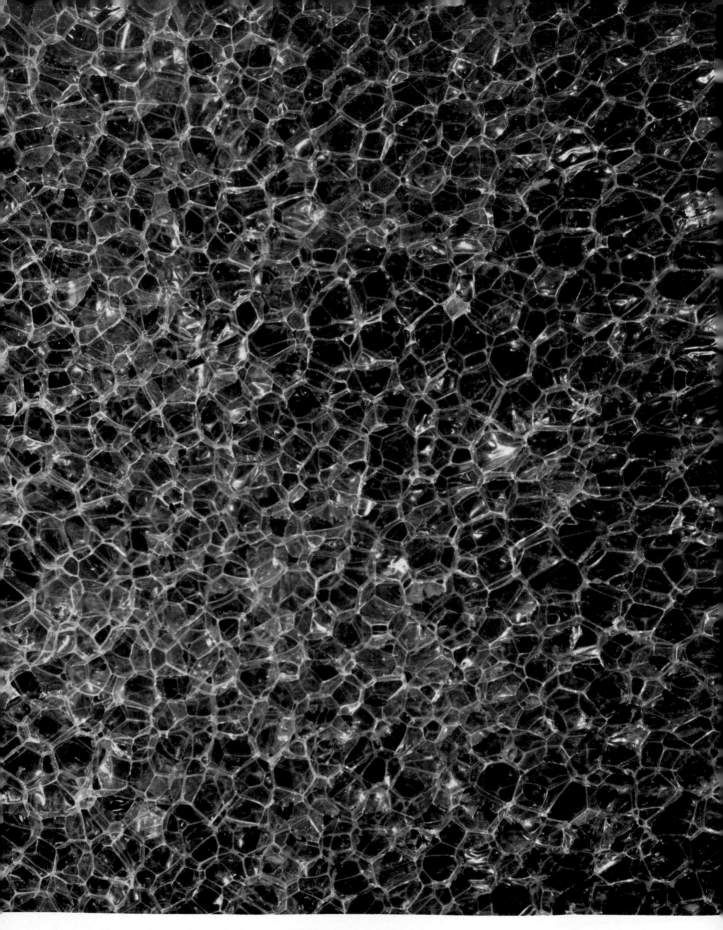

D112   Plastic bubbles, used as experimental material.
Side lighting. Reduced to ½ actual size.

INDEX

INDEX